Presented to

_____

By

_____

On the Occasion of

_____

Date

_____

A TEACHER'S HEART

COLLEEN L. REECE
AND
ANITA CORRINE DONIHUE

BARBOUR
PUBLISHING, INC.
Uhrichsville, Ohio

Published by Barbour Publishing, Inc.
P.O. Box 719
Uhrichsville, Ohio 44683
http://www.barbourbooks.com

Member of the
Evangelical Christian
Publishers Association

Printed in the United States of America.

Admonition

Train a child in the way he should go,
and when he is old he will not turn from it.
PROVERBS 22:6, NIV

Achievement

Successful teachers are those who have lived well,
laughed often, and loved much;
who have gained the respect of intelligent persons
and the love of children;
who have filled their niches and accomplished their tasks;
who leave the world better than they found it—
whether by an improved poppy,
a perfect poem, or a rescued soul;
who never lacked appreciation of earth's beauty
or failed to express it;
who looked for the best in others
and gave the best they had.

Adapted from ROBERT LOUIS STEVENSON

A Teacher's Heart

A teacher's heart has many rooms.
Each needs a different key.
Love and caring unbolt some compartments.
Faith and prayer find a way into others.
Patience and compassion pick the locks
of tightly shuttered windows,
letting in the light of hope and encouragement.
Only then can lives be changed; teachers' and students',
Forever.

A teacher's heart has many rooms.
Each needs a different key,
designed by the Master Teacher
who made the shores of the Sea of Galilee
His classroom and changed the world,
Forever.

A CHILD SMILES
AND CHASES AWAY
THE GRAY
OF A TEACHER'S DAY.

Inner Vision

If you could see beneath the rumpled hair,
The pizza-stained shirt, behind the freckles.
If you could look inside a squirming body;
Dreamy eyes staring out the window,
What would you find?
A second Einstein? Another Michelangelo?
Or a child like every other child,
Longing for you to turn the key;
To set him free to become what he longs to be.

Children of the Heavenly Father

Children of the heavenly Father
Safely in His bosom gather;
Nestling bird nor star in heaven
Such a refuge e'er was given.
Though He giveth or He taketh,
God His children ne'er forsaketh;
His the loving purpose solely
To preserve them pure and holy.

CAROLINE V. SANDELL BERG, 1855

IF YOU CAN BRING
ONE MOMENT OF
HAPPINESS INTO THE LIFE
OF A CHILD,
YOU ARE A CO-WORKER
WITH GOD.

It takes a special kind of love,
the patience of Job,
and the wisdom of Solomon to
parent, teach, and minister to children with special needs.
Yet even small triumphs bring
great joy and affirm that
such efforts are worthwhile.

*And whoever welcomes
a little child like this in my name
welcomes me.*
MATTHEW 18:5, NIV

I Love You Special

The first time I met seven-year-old Lacey, she stole my heart. Her long, blond ponytail bounced behind her, reflecting her bubbly personality. Her blue eyes sparkled from behind thick, heavy glasses. And I soon learned that her sparsely-toothed grin is a smile that doesn't quit.

Lacey has Down's Syndrome. In spite of her difficulty in learning quickly, she is curious and eager to try. She ran so fast during recess I could barely keep up. Everyone marveled at the way she performed flips and turns on the monkey bars. Friends from all classes flocked to her. Sometimes Lacey was overwhelmed and covered her eyes until I helped her escape from so much excitement. Before she did, she always hugged the other students, whom she genuinely loved.

Unlike the other kids, Lacey never called me Mrs. Donihue or Mrs. D.; she's always called me "Teach." At times she could be stubborn. Arms and legs crossed on the rug, she would refuse to do her work, but her pout would soon leave and her irresistible smile return.

After three years with us, Lacey moved on to another school. I could barely contain the tears when we said good-bye. We had developed a special kind of love.

Lacey still has a corner of my heart. I keep her picture up and pray for her. Occasionally, she returns to visit our class. And one of my biggest thrills is when I'm in a store or restaurant and hear her unmistakable strong, husky voice call, "Hey, Teach!"

The world around us seems to stop. Lacey dashes toward me and I brace myself. Arms and legs fly around my waist and neck in a vise-like hug that I joyfully return. Then I hear the words that warm and melt my heart. "I love you, Teach. I love you special."

I am here for a purpose.
I came from heaven above
With something great to give you:
A special kind of love

May we open
our hearts
and let that love shine in.

Following Stars

Ralph Waldo Emerson said, " Hitch your wagon to a star." The Three Wise Men probably had no wagon, but they followed the Star of the East. It led them to the world's greatest treasure, Jesus, lying in a manger near Bethlehem. Surely God smiles when dedicated teachers encourage their students to follow their own particular stars.

Did They Know?

Did the disciples know as they sat at Jesus' feet and learned life's most important lessons, that one day they would pick up the torch of his teachings and carry light into a dark world?

What teachers instill in young minds is the spark from which generations of flaming torches of truth may be lit.

Heart and Spirit

At six weeks of age, she became ill. Doctors seriously and tragically erred in her treatment. As a result, she lost her eyesight and could only distinguish darkness from light.

In spite of her disability, her parents and teachers encouraged her to try as many things as possible during childhood. She loved to climb trees and ride horses bareback. Remarkably, she memorized huge portions of the Bible. Later, she studied at the Northwest Institute for the Blind, then remained at the school to teach history and language.

She weighed no more than a hundred pounds as a young lady. Not attractive by conventional standards, her wit, grace, and charm captured listeners when she spoke. Her compassion for the needy, for street people, and for children made her lovely in heart and spirit.

Her music and poetry filled our world. She wrote between 8000 and 9000 hymns and at seventy-one, penned one of her best-loved hymns, "Saved by Grace." Her name was Fanny Crosby.

Father, help us all to
see beyond our limitations.
Every man's life is a fairy tale
written by God's fingers.

HANS CHRISTIAN ANDERSEN

Hans Christian Andersen was the son of a poor shoemaker in Denmark who died when Hans was eleven years old. He attended the Odense city school for poor children. Later a friend helped him get a scholarship to continue his education.

Was it there he first began to write? To observe life and weave moral teachings into his fairy tales, plays, and novels? Perhaps. Who can forget the excitement when first hearing how "The Ugly Duckling" (based on Andersen's own life) became a glorious swan? Or how Hans poked fun at persons who thought too highly of themselves by penning "The Emperor's New Clothes"?

Generations of adults and children continue to enjoy and learn from Hans Christian Andersen's work.

Pebble on the Shore

I do not know what I may appear to the world;
but to myself I seem to have been only
like a boy playing on the seashore,
and diverting myself in now and then
finding a smoother pebble or a pretty shell,
whilst the great ocean of truth lay
all undiscovered before me.

SIR ISAAC NEWTON

Once a Teacher, Always a Teacher

Mom found her many years of teaching elementary school invaluable even after she retired. She saw examples for life in even the smallest incidents.

One day our large orange and white cat clawed at the screen door and meowed.

Mom went to see what he wanted. There stood Felix (who in no way resembled the cartoon cat) proudly displaying his hunting prowess.

Mom gingerly disposed of the dead mouse, patted Felix and exclaimed, "What a good cat you are!" He trotted at her heels, wearing a satisfied cat-smirk on his babyish face.

The next day Felix summoned her to view a dead mole, the results of his hunting in the vacant lot next to our house. Mom was impressed and said so.

The third day Felix went through the same rigmarole. Mom was beginning to tire of his rodent offerings. Which would it be today? Mouse or mole? She took one look and shook with laughter. Mighty hunter Felix had brought her a long and wiggling night crawler!

Mom didn't have the heart to erase the self-satisfied smile from his smug face. The cat got his petting and praise.

When she told me about it that night, she held her sides from laughing. "Isn't that just like some people?" she gasped when she could get her breath. "As proud of a tiny achievement as a large one."

I thought of times I had visited Mom's classroom. I'd seen shocky-headed urchins walk away from their teacher's desk, heads high, eyes shining. "Yes," I agreed. "But remember, you always praised your students' efforts equally, the same way you praised Felix for his mouse, mole, and night crawler. The child who showed the slightest improvement received the same warm approval as those making A's. And that's why they all loved you."

Mom just smiled.

The orange and white cat in her lap shot me a triumphant glance and purred louder than ever.

Point to Ponder

Yesterday is only a memory,
tomorrow a hope.
Today is ours.

Be prepared in season and out of season. . .
2 TIMOTHY 4:2, NIV

Words

If there be words of kindness
words of praise
words of encouragement
speak them now.
Listen to your heart and respond.
Someone, somewhere, is waiting for your words.

Lost Opportunities

A teacher once thought she would write and congratulate a co-worker on a special achievement. Instead, she grew busy and failed to do so. She excused herself by saying her letter would never be missed in the wealth of congratulations the other teacher would be sure to receive.

Some time later, she met her fellow instructor and apologized. To her amazement and dismay, the hardworking teacher had not received even one congratulatory note of commendation or appreciation.

John Ruskin once said two sad things happen when we fail to praise. We run the risk of driving a person from the right road for want of encouragement, and we deprive ourselves of the happy privilege of rewarding deserving labor.

Lord, may we always be quick to praise,
slow to criticize.

GENIUS IS
UNDISCOVERED GOLD.
TALENTED IS
THE TEACHER WHO
STRUGGLES, FINDS, AND
HELPS STUDENTS
DEVELOP IT.

Harvey

Everybody loved Harvey. Although he worked slowly, he faithfully cleaned the classrooms and hallways at Parker Senior High. Every time you saw Harvey, he had something cheerful to say to a student. His best quality was being a good listener. While he scrubbed walls and windows, Harvey listened and nodded as one student after another unloaded his concerns.

One day someone discovered Harvey's 50th birthday was coming up. The news spread like a forest fire. The students collected money and the school decided to hold an assembly. The office paged Harvey to the auditorium, asking him to "clean up a mess" there. Moments later he walked into the auditorium carrying a mop and a bucket.

The senior class president stood and asked, "Harvey, would you please come to the platform?"

Harvey slowly came forward.

The president smiled. "On behalf of the student body, I am honored to present you with your very own Parker Senior High jacket." He held out a package.

Overwhelmed, eyes brimming, the beloved custodian took the gift and choked out a thank you.

The students cheered. "Yeah, Harvey! Happy birthday! We love you!"

Harvey continued cleaning and listening to students. And he proudly wore his jacket every day.

Lord,
help us to always show
appreciation to
those around us.

Opportunity

They do me wrong,
who say I come no more,
When once I knock
and fail to find you in;
For every day I stand
outside your door,
And bid you wake,
and rise to fight and win.

WALTER MALONE

Looking Up

Far away there in the sunshine
are my highest aspirations.
I may not reach them,
but I can look up and see their beauty,
believe in them,
and try to follow where they lead.

LOUISA MAY ALCOTT

*In all these things we are
more than conquerors
through him who loved us.*
ROMANS 8:37, NIV

> The man without purpose is
> like a ship without a rudder—a waif,
> a nothing, a no man.
> Have a purpose in life, and having it,
> throw such strength of mind and muscle
> into your work as God has given you.

THOMAS CARLYLE

Thomas Carlyle certainly knew adversity. He experienced one of the worst things that can happen to an author. After completing the first volume of his book, *The French Revolution,* his friend John Stuart Mill borrowed the manuscript. By accident, Mill's housemaid burned the manuscript! Carlyle didn't give up, however. He rewrote the book, largely from memory. It was finally published in 1837.

The next time the computer eats your lesson plans, remember Thomas Carlyle!

Learning to Multiply

The first Sunday my husband and I visited our new church, we were made to feel welcome, but something was missing. The tiny congregation, made up mostly of older people, had no children. We knew God had led us to this church. It was plain to see we were needed. Everyone longed to hear the sound of children's laughter echo through the building.

What could I do to help? I already taught school during the week and worked nights at a second job. Still, I felt God's tugging. Could he be leading me to teach the children we hoped would come? Where would I find the physical strength? Most of all, where would the kids come from?

A young mother and her two-year-old daughter Sierra began attending church. Dark, tightly-curled ringlets framed the little girl's warm brown eyes and irresistible smile. I fell hopelessly in love with Sierra. Each time I turned around, she had her arms outstretched, waiting for me to pick her up.

God, there is only this one child, I prayed. *Can we reach more? Please help us multiply into many children.*

The following spring a vision for a Vacation Bible School struck me. And I knew I was the only one who could direct it. And though it was summer vacation, with my second job I would still have to function on four to five hours of sleep each night if I directed the week-long VBS. I prayed for strength and we launched into the program. Some said we couldn't do it, but our church's grandmas and grandpas showed up in force to go door knocking, then mustered their energy and skills and did what was needed. Kids came. We were successful. At the end of the week, we had a church school promotional picnic.

Next came the question: Who would teach the Primary/Junior class? We didn't even have teaching materials. Feeling nudged, I committed to six months. I dug remnants of teaching materials out of storage and poured my heart into the program. Before long we averaged fifteen to twenty kids each week.

Less than a year later, I watched six eager Juniors and one older brother tell of their love for God and be baptized. I was so happy I cried and thanked God.

Now the once-quiet halls of our church ring with children's laughter after worship. And when I feel that familiar tug at my skirt, I gather little Sierra into my arms. I can hardly wait for the day she is old enough to join my class, for I will continue teaching. With God's help, not only the children, but my commitment to love and teach has multiplied.

Duty Bound and
Honor Bound

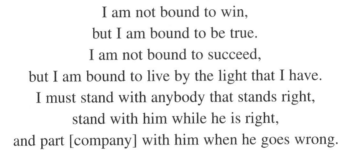

I am not bound to win,
but I am bound to be true.
I am not bound to succeed,
but I am bound to live by the light that I have.
I must stand with anybody that stands right,
stand with him while he is right,
and part [company] with him when he goes wrong.

ABRAHAM LINCOLN

From Seed to Harvest

Ben entered the huge multipurpose room of the church where the Christian Education conference was to be held. Electrical zeal and enthusiasm filled the air and Ben sensed the unmistakable presence of the Lord. But even after thirty years, he loyally clung to the small-town church where he taught church school.

A handsome middle-aged man eagerly approached Ben and smothered him in a bear hug. His humble, tender gaze searched the elderly teacher's face. His voice cracked and tears glistened in his eyes. "How are you, Ben? I am so happy to see you," he said.

Ben gripped Randy's hands. Looking at the face of the caring, dynamic pastor, Ben could still see that of a troubled teen. He remembered how thirty years earlier, Randy had almost lost sight of his calling to the ministry, how a friend's new red convertible and successful job had tempted the student facing mid-college burnout. Randy knew that if he left college, he would have plenty of money and he could trade in that old Volkswagon for a better car.

Then God led Ben to spend hours with the troubled young man. After intense prayer, Randy exchanged material desires and regained his vision for God's ministry. He continued his studies and became what God wanted him to be: A caring, dynamic pastor, whose congregation numbered more than 5000.

Influence

He who is firm in will,
moulds the world to himself.

JOHANN WOLFGANG VON GOETHE

Fly Ball

Eight-year-old Anthony watched the kids play kickball. Anthony cheered and clapped his hands. Each time there was a catch, kick, or home run, he strained at his wheelchair seat belt, clapping and kicking with excitement. How he longed to be in that game!

Then it happened. The ball landed smack in Anthony's lap. He grabbed it with both hands. His brown eyes glowed and a bright smile lit up his face. Although he couldn't speak, Anthony showed what he could do. With a mighty heave, he sailed the ball across the diamond to home base!

The other kids were shocked, then excited. They all cheered wildly. Everyone knew Anthony loved ball games. He went to pro baseball games with his family and watched every game he could on TV. But what the kids didn't know was that Anthony and his dad spent many hours together playing catch in the park and in the family's backyard.

Soon Anthony was made pitcher. He not only pitched well, he put several people out. When his turn came to kick, one of the other kids helped him. Then Anthony flew from base to base in his wheelchair while his team cheered him on.

Even though the game went a little slower, everyone—especially Anthony—had more fun and all showed good team spirit. If you ask, you'll find that Anthony and his team are always ready for another game.

There never shall be
one lost good.
All we have willed or hoped
or dreamed of good
shall exist.

ROBERT BROWNING

Story behind the Painting "The Praying Hands"

Albrecht Durer longed to draw and paint, but he came from a poor family in Germany. His older friend also wanted to become a great artist and suggested they live together. They struggled to earn enough to put food on the table, so Durer's friend said, "I will make our living. When your paintings begin to sell, I will have my chance." He waved away Durer's protests. "I have a job in a restaurant. I am also older and have not so much talent. You must not waste your years." The friend worked long hours, planning for the wonderful day he would be free to pursue his goal.

Albrecht studied hard. At last he sold a wood carving. "Now I shall be the breadwinner," he declared. "Go to your paints, my friend."

The older man took up his brush. Alas for his dreams. Years of hard work had twisted his hands. He could no longer hold the brush with mastery and skill.

Albrecht Durer found his friend in prayer, hands clasped. Durer could not give back the lost skill, but his wonderful painting "The Praying Hands" captures the spirit of a noble, unselfish man who sacrificed his dreams to help another.

Slowing Down

The end of the world
does not depend on whether
we cleaned house or
washed dirty windows today.
We just think it does!

Work first, then rest.

JOHN RUSKIN

Foolish persons take better care
of their cars than of themselves.
Wise persons know they may have
many cars in their lifetimes,
but only one body.

39

Seven Simple Ways
to Reduce Stress

1. A quiet, private devotion during recess.

2. A brisk walk before or after school, or at noon.

3. A warm cup of tea, any time.

4. A quick stretch.

5. A change of classroom routine.

6. Drive to or from work a different way.

7. Imagine you are in Hawaii!

Actions Speak

Every week James delivered his son to church school, drove home, picked up his wife, and returned in time for eleven o'clock service. One sunny morning when they pulled up in front of the church, young Jimmy crossed his arms, stuck out his lower lip, and announced, "I ain't going."

"Of course you are," James exclaimed. "Go on, son."

Jimmy shook his head violently and stuck his lip out farther. "Naw. If it ain't good enough for you, it ain't good enough for me."

The next week, the whole family attended church school.

Actions really do speak louder than words.

He who doubts is like a wave of the sea,
blown and tossed by the wind.
JAMES 1:6, NIV

Handle With Care

Ten-year-old Brian strolled into church school and slipped into his seat. Kris launched into her lesson with fervor and enthusiasm. The kids all responded well, yet each time she glanced at Brian, he appeared deep in thought.

Months passed. Each week the questions flew, especially from Brian. Kris took each question seriously, wondering what was going on in this special boy's head. One morning Kris asked if any of the kids knew what he or she wanted to do in the future. Some gave guesses or dreams, but no doubt clouded Brian's eyes.

"I'm going to be a preacher," he announced matter-of-factly. His clear, steady gaze met his teacher's, showing wisdom beyond his years. "That's why I want to learn so much. I know it's what I'm supposed to do."

Kris turned to Bible study and prayer to discover how she could best help Brian. The answers she received were simple: Handle with care. Don't expect more or less from him than anyone else. Don't use him as an example. Just teach him all he wants to learn, then show him how he can develop a close, growing, and personal relationship

with his Lord. Hold him up in daily prayer. Be there when he needs to talk. Then step back and let the Lord work directly in Brian's life.

Jesus . . . said to them,
"Let the little children come to me,
and do not hinder them,
for the kingdom of God
belongs to such as these."
MARK 10:14, KJV

What Were Jesus' Teachers Like?

What were they like, those long-ago persons who taught Jesus?

Did Joseph teach Him songs, psalms, and passages from the Torah? Did he teach lessons traditionally passed from father to son? Did he place tiny Jesus on a stool to learn the carpenter trade? Or give Him livelihood skills? Surely he exhibited unfaltering faith in the One true God, strength to love and protect Jesus by God's directions.

What about Mary? Did she share with Jesus what God had revealed to her, or hold her secrets within, letting the boy discover His own answers from God? Perhaps she showed him nature's miracles and taught Him to respect the beauty, dangers, and frailty in plants and animals. Did His mother model gentleness, love, responsibility? Did she teach Jesus geography while balancing Him on her hip, naming the Plain of Esdraelon, the Jordan valley? Did His keen gaze follow her pointing finger across the valley to Mount Carmel, or the closer Mt. Tabor?

How did she describe the waves, the breeze, the many storms on the Sea of Galilee? Did Jesus see His mother frown when she spoke of sharp pyramids and the Sphinx? Her eyes would have sparkled when she painted word pictures of the Mount of Olives, Jerusalem, and of the beloved temple. Her longing to return to the sacred place of worship must have been contagious.

As Jesus grew, did His mother ever correct Him? In learning to obey her and Joseph, Jesus surely learned unquestioning obedience to His Heavenly Father.

Who were His grandparents? Was Jesus close to them? Did they instill priceless wisdom, exhibiting by their lives a zest for life Jesus could mirror? Perhaps they taught him patience and the ability to speak out for truth and righteousness.

His teachers in the synagogue may have been kind and caring, or stern and aloof. Either way, the rabbis must have opened to Jesus the mysteries in God's Word, by insisting on perfection from the Christ Child as He memorized passage after passage. When he challenged their teachings, they had no idea He was the Son of God—although they marveled at His perception. If they had accepted Jesus' challenges, they would have poured their entire knowledge into Him, heart and soul, seeing light and hope for the future even in One so young.

What did the shepherds teach Jesus? Did He see how they were willing to lay down their lives for their sheep? Were they unknowingly

preparing Him to someday become the Good Shepherd?

Journeying to Jerusalem for the Passover as a twelve-year-old reinforced Jesus' lessons in history and geography. Storytellers among His fellow travelers undoubtedly predicted the coming of the Messiah.

Did His Aunt Elisabeth teach Jesus? Did she share any secrets she had learned twelve years before? Or did she, too, keep silent? What if the family could have seen beyond the meager sacrifice of the roasted Paschal lamb and seen the true Lamb of God?

What was the high priest in the temple like? Did the promise he and the wise elders discerned in Jesus make them feel threatened, without knowing why?

What did Jesus learn from His Heavenly Father, in early-morning solitude and prayer? We cannot know if or when the Author and Finisher, Teacher above all teachers, laid the eternal plan of salvation before the boy-man Jesus, step by painful step. Did God expect His Son to unconditionally obey? Did He reveal to Jesus how the supreme sacrifice would explode in holy triumph, victory, and eternal life for all who believed and accepted?

Did even one of Jesus' earthly teachers suspect who they taught? Were any, other than God, worthy to guide His only Son?

Someone Who Cared

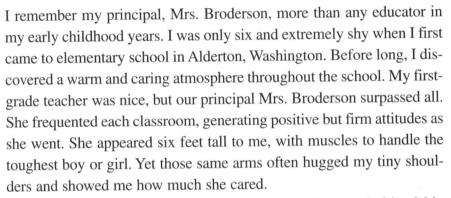

I remember my principal, Mrs. Broderson, more than any educator in my early childhood years. I was only six and extremely shy when I first came to elementary school in Alderton, Washington. Before long, I discovered a warm and caring atmosphere throughout the school. My first-grade teacher was nice, but our principal Mrs. Broderson surpassed all. She frequented each classroom, generating positive but firm attitudes as she went. She appeared six feet tall to me, with muscles to handle the toughest boy or girl. Yet those same arms often hugged my tiny shoulders and showed me how much she cared.

Our principal insisted on manners, equality, and friendship among all the children, no matter our background or race. Patriotism ranked high and we learned the songs of our country well. Mrs. Broderson made recess fun, with a teacher always ready to rescue us, as needed.

At lunch time, we gathered in small groups around long tables. A teacher stood at one end. We were asked to wait until everyone at our table was served before we ate. Then the teacher motioned for silence while she prayed the blessing on us and our food. We said, "Please,"

and "Thank you," and we asked "May I be excused?" before we left the table.

Mrs. Broderson's lessons followed me into adulthood. She armed me with three vital ingredients for life: love for God, self-control, and a good self-esteem. In turn, I carried these lessons over into daycare centers I taught and directed. Now I am in a public school, but the teacher I work with and I pray silently before meals. We still plant seeds of love, kindness, and self-esteem. We still care and pray for each student.

Thank you, Mrs. Broderson, for all you did for me.

*Goodness is the only investment
that never fails.*

HENRY DAVID THOREAU

You Never Know

The story is told of a doctor in Wales who was called to care for a desperately ill child on a terrible night. Devotion to duty and love for God's children forced him to brave one of the worst storms the countryside had ever seen and respond to the call. Years later, the child he saved rose to high places. Many times the old doctor shook his head and marveled. There had been no way for him to know the far-reaching effects of his actions. He had faced the wild storm to care for the child of a widowed mother, a child he believed would become a common laborer.

In so doing, the doctor actually saved the life of a future Prime Minister.

Even Great Men Can Be Wrong

"The world will little note,
nor long remember what we say here,
but it can never forget what they
the brave men, living and dead did here."

ABRAHAM LINCOLN
"The Gettysburg Address"

Lincoln was wrong. His words will be remembered as long as there are history books, encyclopedias, and wise teachers to pass them on.

The full impact of words spoken from a teacher's heart is seldom recognized by the one who speaks, or at the time the words are given. Yet after many years, students may well look back and call those who cared blessed.

The Coat

After Fran's older sister died, Fran donated most of her clothing to a charitable organization. One of the few items she kept was The Coat. The two women had found it at an incredible sale. "I'll only be wearing it in the coldest weather," she had commented. "It will last me for the rest of my life." Her eyes sparkled. "You can borrow it, Fran."

"Thanks," she'd said. Remembering this, love swept through Fran, and thankfulness for the many years she and Joy had spent together. Just touching it brought happy memories of Joy's laughing face against the warmly lined hood. Although it wasn't her best color, Fran wore The Coat after Joy died. Its plush folds wrapped around her like loving arms.

A year later, Fran thought of a new teacher friend going through hard times. Would Susan feel insulted if she offered her the rest of Joy's clothing?

A startling thought came: Give Susan Joy's coat. "What? It's my warmest coat, and it brings back memories of Joy," she protested.

Susan needs it more than you do, a small inner voice whispered.

Fran felt like a wishbone. "Even though it's in good condition, offering Susan an old coat might hurt her feelings, Lord. Besides, maybe I'm just looking for an excuse to buy a new one!" A bright idea came. "How about a test? If I'm supposed to give Susan The Coat, help me find a replacement for . . . (she named a ridiculously low figure). A few hours later, she found a warmly lined raincoat at less than half the full price, and far below her stated limit.

That evening Susan dropped by Fran's house. Fran brought out two almost-new sweatshirts. "Can you use a few things?" Susan's face lit up, so Fran added, "There's one more thing. It isn't new, though." She took The Coat from a closet.

Susan blinked, swallowed hard and bowed her head.

Fran felt terrible. Despite her prayers and precautions, she had misinterpreted her own feelings for God's directions. How could she have been so mistaken?

Susan looked up. Her lips quivered. "This is a direct answer to prayer. For weeks I've been praying for a warm winter coat, but didn't know how it was possible."

May we always appreciate our blessings as much as Susan appreciated The Coat.

He that hath two coats, let him impart to him that hath none . . .
LUKE 3:11, KJV

Who's the Teacher?

Paul always tried to bring Bible stories alive so the kids in his junior high church school class could get to know real people from long ago. He loved his students and they reciprocated. Paul also wanted to pour as much as possible into their bright minds during their few short years together, to prepare them for the future.

One gorgeous spring morning, Paul told his class about Rachel, and the inspiring life of Joseph. He was totally caught up in the events and on a roll. When Jason's hand shot up, Paul gently reminded, "Just a minute," and continued the story.

Jason's hand popped up again and again, with Paul responding the same way. When the boy waved his hand wildly, the teacher sighed and said," Yes, Jason?"

Jason rapidly traced his finger through the pages of his Bible. "Do you know Jacob and Joseph are great-great relatives of Jesus?" He raised one fist high, with a "Yes!"

"This is so cool!" The other kids chimed in.

Paul suddenly realized his kids were teachers, too. He saw the future budding in them like the spring growth outside the window. From then on, his class was never the same. He had discovered some teachers in the making.

A Heart-Felt Prayer
for Teachers

Lord, please bless all teachers.
Those who serve in public schools,
in private schools, through homeschooling.
And those who teach Your Word
in weekly church school classes.

All have chosen the paths
for which they feel they are best suited.
All have chosen the paths they feel
will best serve those they endeavor to teach.

Guide their feet that they may not stumble or lose the way,
lest those following after lose sight of the goal
and settle for a little knowledge when much is needed.

Help them instill in young hearts and minds
seeds of greatness, seeds of honor,
seeds of compassion, seeds of tolerance,
seeds of courage to stand for what is right and denounce the wrong,
no matter how high the cost may be for speaking out.

Lord, please bless all teachers.
You have given them
the responsibility of training those who must grasp the future.
May it not be with uncertain hands, but with confidence.
May those You have called to point the way
first learn it from Thee.

Do your best to present yourself to God as one approved,
a workman who does not need to be ashamed and
who correctly handles the word of truth.
2 TIMOTHY 2:15, KJV

Two Builders

A builder builded a temple;
He wrought with care and skill;
Pillars and groins and arches
Were fashioned to meet his will;

And men said when they saw its beauty
"It shall never know decay.
Great is thy skill, oh builder,
Thy fame shall endure for aye."

A teacher builded a temple;
She wrought with skill and care;
Forming each pillar with patience,
Laying each stone with prayer.

None saw the unceasing effort;
None knew of the marvelous plan;
For the temple the teacher builded
Was unseen by the eyes of man.

Gone is the builder's temple;
Crumbled into the dust,
Pillar and groin and arches
Food for consuming rust;

But the temple the teacher builded
Shall endure while the ages roll;
For that beautiful, unseen temple
Was a Child's immortal soul.

AUTHOR UNKNOWN

Sometimes when I am lonely, or discouraged, or sad, I withdraw from even my closest friends. I turn to others who have also touched my life: my book friends. They demand nothing from me but a little time. They welcome me into their worlds and include me in mental vacations my body is too busy to take. The Maine coast in summer. The Sea of Galilee, where Jesus walked. Magnificent mountains in Alaska. The magic of childhood revisited. A way of life now gone.

Knowing my book friends will always be there when I need them is a precious part of my life. I close a treasured book, return from my visit refreshed, and eagerly, joyously, look forward to meeting my book friends again.

I would rather be a poor man
in a garret with plenty of books
than a king who did not love reading.

THOMAS BARBINGTON MACAULAY

A Race to the Finish

Kelly stood near nine-year-old Manuel's wheelchair during noon recess. Only a week of school remained, so all the classroom balls and other playground equipment were checked in. Kelly's students wondered what they could do.

"Why don't you run races to the fence (a distance of about two blocks) and back?" she suggested. "Get ready. Get set. Go!" Off ran a half dozen kids.

Manuel watched longingly. He couldn't walk or speak, though he signed a little. Now he motioned for his teacher to help him out of his chair and onto the grass. Several of Manuel's good fifth grade friends joined him. Manual looked as though he desperately wanted to race with the other kids. He glanced up at Kelly and they exchanged smiles.

Julie, a mother helper, happened along just then. "He wants to be in the race more than anything," Kelly told Julie. A few minutes later, Kelly said, "Well, look at that! He's going to give it a try." She felt surprised and thrilled. Manuel crawled about six feet across the grass and turned for her approval. Kelly nodded and gave him a big smile. Soon his fifth grade friends joined him. "I can't believe it," Kelly exclaimed. "They're pacing him!"

Manuel reached the halfway point. Kelly glanced at her watch and turned to Julie. "Will you please get Manuel while I gather the other kids?" Julie started across the play yard. The look on Manuel's face showed pure determination.

I don't care if we're late getting in, Kelly decided. *This is more important.* She motioned the group on. More kids entered the race, walking at Manuel's speed.

They finally reached the fence. Manuel turned and started back. Sometimes he flopped on the grass. The others flopped with him. Then he was on his way again. Soon all his friends were on their knees crawling along with him. Julie walked at Manuel's side. Kelly and other students cheered when he approached the finish line back where he had started. He grinned as though he had completed a marathon. His brown eyes snapped with excitement.

Kelly bent down and helped him step carefully to his chair. His little legs trembled. "Manuel, I'm so proud of you!" She gathered his small body in her arms and placed him in his chair while everyone clapped.

Manuel looked proud and thrilled. He'd finished the race and knew he'd won!

Who Am I?

Who am I, Lord, to teach children?
There is so much I do not know.
How can I teach the importance of loving?
I struggle so.

Lord, may my students always see
The real teaching come from Thee.

*Love conquers all things; let us too
surrender to love.*

VIRGIL

Motto on a Sun Dial:

"I only mark the hours that shine."

At the end of a tough day,
deliberately focusing on the shining hours
or moments can bring peace, rest,
and the will to go on.

Teach Me,
My God and King

Teach me, my God and King,
In all things thee to see;
Teach me to be in everything
All thou wouldst have me be.

In all I think or say, Lord,
may I not offend.
In all I do, be thou the way;
In all be thou the end.

Each task I undertake,
Though weak and mean to me,
If undertaken for thy sake
Draws strength and worth from thee.

Teach me, then, Lord, to bring
To all that I may be,
To all I do, my God and King,
A consciousness of thee.

GEORGE HERBERT

I have fought the good fight,
I have finished the race,
I have kept the faith.
2 TIMOTHY 4:7, NIV